# Voices From The Silence

Deslee Campbell

Published by Deslee Campbell, 2024.

VOICES FROM THE SILENCE

**First edition. May 23, 2024.**

Copyright © 2024 Deslee Campbell.

ISBN: 979-8215152904

Written by Deslee Campbell.

# Table of Contents

# Chapter 1

What Holocaust?

ON THE FIRST OF VERY many visits to Yad Vashem, the Holocaust Martyrs' and Heroes' Remembrance Authority in Jerusalem I was accompanied by a Australian woman I had just met. When I told her that this place was a memorial to the Holocaust she said "What Holocaust?" She was a tourist in Israel, yet she had only the most minimal perception of what Hitler had done, in decimating the World's Jewish population, in exterminating, by various means, two thirds of the Jews of Europe and one fifth of the Jews of the entire world.

Despite the claims of the vocal few who say that the Holocaust never happened, (but is a Jewish invention to deceive the world, extract compensation payments from Germany, and legitimise the State of Israel) serious scholars continue to amass the evidence. The six years of the Second World War, of which the Holocaust is a vital part, is the most thoroughly documented and critically researched period of world history, in the annals of humankind. Even after 75 years this painstaking research continues; given new impetus with the release of the vast mass of documentation from former Soviet archives, kept hidden for so many years.

A representative list of facts and dates are critical as background to an understanding of the Jewish Holocaust. This list shows how early in the Third Reich the concentration camps were established, that anti-Jewish laws preceded the outbreak of War, and that an extermination camp was built and trialled before the `Final Solution of the Jewish Problem' was approved as official policy.

Jan '33 Adolf Hitler was elected German Chancellor

Mar '33 Dachau camp established

Aug '34 Hitler became dictator of Germany, legally

Sep '35 Nuremberg Laws: Jews civil rights denied

Jul '37 Buchenwald Camp established

Mar '38 Hitler annexed Austria

Aug '38 Attacks on synagogues & against Jews

Nov '38 Kristallnacht pogroms in Germany

Mar '39 Nazis invaded Czechoslovakia & Lithuania

Sep '39 Poland invaded. Allies declared war

Oct '39 Jews property seized, Ghettoisation begun

Jun '41 Shooting squads scour captured Soviet lands

Oct '41 Birkenau (Auschwitz II) built

Nov '41 Belzec Extermination Camp built & used

Jan '42 Final Solution formulated, Nazi leaders agree

Sep '42 Battle of Stalingrad, the tide turns

Dec '42 Allies condemn "cold blooded extermination"

Feb '43 Gipsy Camp at Auschwitz opened

Oct '43 Rescue of Danish Jews to Sweden

May '44 Mass murder of Hungarian Jews in Auschwitz

Jun '44 D-Day Allied Landing in France

Jul '44 First death march, from Warsaw

Sep '44 Soviets liberate Klooga camp, 85 Jews alive

Jan '45 Soviets liberate Auschwitz, 7,650 Jews alive

Apr '45 Allies liberate Buchenwald & Bergen-Belsen

Apr '45 Hitler suicides

May '45 Victory in Europe Day

Sep '45 Japanese surrender. Victory in the Pacific

---

A NUMBER OF ITEMS AT the Yad Vashem Memorial illustrate the significance of these world-shattering events. The Valley of the Destroyed Communities commemorates the villages and shtetles of Europe, whose entire populations were obliterated without trace. The Hall of Names records as many of the personal details of those who died as surviving friends or relatives can remember: two million names have been recorded so far. The huge six branch Memorial Candelabra, lit each year on Yom Hashoah, Holocaust Memorial Day, represents the estimated six million victims. The darkness of the powerfully moving Children's Memorial, lit by a million tiny reflections of one candle, is a tribute to the children who were lost for all their generations to come. The museum houses Torah Scrolls and religious memorabilia, rescued from destroyed synagogues; and survivor Elsa Pollock's sculpture, a large pile of assorted shoes, reminds us all of the human dimensions: baby shoes, fashion shoes, men's old work boots, right feet, left feet, broken shoelaces....

# Chapter 2

---

Two Girls, Two Boys

This is the story of four teenagers. It does not begin "once upon a time" because it is not make believe. It is not fiction. No fiction could be as bizarre, or as tragic, as this story. It is beyond the power of human imagination, of human comprehension: and yet it is true, it is fact, it is history.

There is no "happily ever after" ending, no fairy princess or handsome prince to marry them, nor even to take them to the ball. None of the four lived to see their eighteenth birthday, let alone their twenty-first. The Great Silence overtook them in the midst of youth - Hitler's gigantic and insane plan to destroy every Jewish man, woman and child from off the face of Europe.

"Death hath climbed in through our windows"

This is the story of four exceptionally gifted young people, two girls: Eva Heyman and Anne Frank; and two boys: Moshe Flinker and Yitskhok Rudashevski. They were overtaken by the silence of death, all four teenagers perished in the great Nazi Holocaust, yet, through their diaries, they still speak to us across the years. Their pens were mightier than the swords, and the guns of death.

Three of these teenagers are virtually unknown, but the name of one has become a household word. Anne Frank is widely featured in movies and writings and her former hiding place has become a mecca for tourists, perhaps even a shrine. Anne Frank's diary has become a set textbook for school examinations, and Anne has become a symbol of moral fortitude, upheld before children throughout the westernised world as an example of youthful human virtue and courage.

Anne's enigmatic 'Mona Lisa smile' is a well-known image, but she is not more worthy of our respect than the other three, her fellow 13 year old diarist, Eva Heyman, and the two boys, Moshe (Moses) Flinker and Yitskhok (Isaac) Rudashevski. Each is a worthy example to inspire any young person living in challenging and dangerous times.

# Chapter 3

Why Read ?

As I write these words, in November 1993, I remember that it is 54 years since 'Kristallnacht', the Night of the Broken Glass, in Hitler's Germany. This was the night when a stunned but fearful world first caught a glimpse of the orchestrated persecution of law abiding Jewish citizens.

Yes the world was stunned, and it did nothing. Within a few years it was too late to act; as the Protestant Holocaust- martyr Dietrich Bonhoeffer said:

"When they came for the Jews, I was not a Jew so I did nothing. When they came for the communists, I was not a communist so I did nothing. When they came for the Catholics, I was not a Catholic so I did nothing. Now they have come for Protestants, it is too late to do anything... "

The unanswerable question is: "How many of the six million Jews who died at the hands of the Nazis would have survived if every nation in the world, and every citizen of each nation, had done everything humanly possible to prevent the genocide?" The war began in 1939. Before the end of 1944, each of the adolescents in this story was already dead.

The heart or emotions, and the mind with its thoughts, perceptions and knowledge, are intimately connected and together constitute the personality. This "inner man" is revealed by actions and speech, and by creative works, such as art works, music and writings. The creative works of those who perished in the Holocaust, are, therefore, a means of discerning the personalities of their creators, as well as discovering how they thought and felt.

Creative art works and music must be interpreted in order to extract their hidden meanings, but plainly written words speak clearly, and, in the personal diary, they speak both honestly and intimately. The personal diary is a window into the soul.

The children's holocaust is the unknown holocaust. Unlike the genocide of the gipsies it is not the forgotten holocaust, because we do remember the one and a half million children who died at the hands of the Nazis between 1933 and 1945, but in many respects their saga remains a mystery. Its magnitude is unknown, and its dimensions unknowable.

Yet it was the children who suffered first and worst. They were the most helpless, yet they were the most in need. They were in need of food, shelter, love and protection; yet their parents were powerless, in their own fear, to adequately provide love and security, and in their own poverty, to provide quality food and shelter. Those who warranted the greatest care, the very old and the very young were the first victims. Their very existence was a liability, even a threat to others. Even to their own communities they were almost dispensable.

On 4th September, 1942 Lodz Ghetto leader Rumkowski in an address to address to the parents of the ghettos' children, defined the harsh realities of those days, and gave voice to the terrible dispensability of the old and the young.

"The Ghetto has been struck a harsh blow. They demand what is most dear to it - children and old people.... I never imagined that my own hands would be forced to make this sacrifice on the altar. In my old age I am forced to stretch out my hands and to beg: Brothers and Sisters, give them to me! - Fathers and Mothers give me your children.... I was given the order to send away more than twenty thousand Jews from the Ghetto...I must cut off limbs in order to save the body!

I must take away children and if I do not, others too will be taken, God forbid." [Documents of the Holocaust (Yad Vashem, 1987), p. 283].

During those terrible years, many children in hiding places were smothered by their terrified parents, and in the camps new-born infants died at their distraught mothers' own hands. There was experimentation on children at Mengele's hands; and slow death by starvation. The children's suffering is unknowable; the bewilderment, loss and hunger they suffered is not recorded. The unborn, aborted in the gas chambers, and the neo-nates who sealed their mothers' fate cannot communicate with us across the years. For these there is not even the mute testimony of a name carved upon some honour board, a gravestone somewhere in the world. Their darkness, darker than that of the Yad Vashem Children's Memorial, cannot be penetrated. Their silence does not speak.

Children's art work and writings therefore stand alone as the only unchanged and original view of the children's own holocaust, albeit a minuscule view of events of horrifying magnitude and monstrous enormity. The unedited diary, written in secret, is as close to the inner life of the child as we can come. A child in extremis does not lie to himself. The few creative works of the young which have survived the Holocaust stand alone as the only original personal testimonies of the children. These four young people, and a handful of others, communicate on behalf of the million and a half whose voice is silent. Their diaries are the stark, unfeigned and original works of the young, delivered, unchanged, to posterity.

These four diarists are representative of Jewish youth during the European Holocaust. All were teenagers. Although all were Jewish, each was raised against a background of different national cultures.

Plate 1. Anne Frank.

Public domain.

They wrote in four different languages and in four different countries of Europe. Although it is in their English translations that their diaries are considered, each of these teenagers was multilingual, literate in up to nine languages. Seventy years onwards, their writings, once so private and secret, can be read by all, to gain some insights into the emotional life and the thoughts of the many, of whom these four are but a minute sample.

Plate 2. Moshe Flinker.

Public domain.

Plate 3 Eva Heyman.

This photo has a copy right claim by Brandnewwta, but is used under the Creative Commons Attribution-Share Alike 4.0 International license.

# Chapter 4



## The Four Diaries

By remarkable coincidence Anne Frank, in Amsterdam, Holland, and Eva Heyman, in Nagyvarad, Hungary, received diaries as gifts for their thirteenth birthdays, and immediately began systematic entries, which continued until their arrest and deportation. In this way the volumes to hand were created at opposite ends of Europe. During the short three and a half month period that Eva was able to write, these diaries were being written simultaneously, both girls' diaries being terminated during the middle part of 1944.

The two male diarists are Moshe Flinker, who commenced writing in Brussels at the end of November 1942, when he was sixteen years old, and Yitskhok Rudashevski, who began to write regularly and systematically in late June of 1941, when he was thirteen and a half years old. Yitskhok's diary was written in Yiddish, in the city of Vilna, which, at first, was in that part of Poland which the U.S.S.R. controlled. A few days after Yitskhok began to write, Vilna fell to the Nazi war machine. This diary covered a period of almost two years, whereas Moshe Flinker's diary, written in Hebrew, covered a period of only ten months.

Factual details of the four diaries, represented on the chart below, indicate their diversity. The similarities of these adolescents include their Jewish designation, their hunted existence, and the untimely ends they each met at the hands of the Nazis.

The diaries fall into natural pairs: into gender groupings (two boys and two girls); and east-west geographic categories. (Anne's and Moshe's diaries were written on the West coast of Europe and Eva's and Yitskhok's were written in East-Central Europe).

| NAME | D.O.B. | AGE | DATES | TIME | LANGUA | CITY |
|---|---|---|---|---|---|---|
| MOSHE FLINKER | 9.10.26 | 16.1-16.11 | 24/11/42-6/9/43 | 10mth | Hebrew | Brus |
| YITSKHOK RUDASHEVS KI | 10.12.27 | 13.7-15.4 | 21/6/41-6/4/43 | 21mth | Yiddish | Vilna |
| ANNE FRANK | 12.6.29 | 13.0-15.1 | 14/6/42-1/8/44 | 25mth | Dutch | Amst |
| EVA HEYMAN | 13.2.31 | 13.0-13.3½ | 13/2/44-30/5/44 | 3½mth | Hungarian | Nagyvara |

On the issue of traditional religion and Jewish lifestyle, the categorisation is less a marked contrast between observant and secular, than a continuum between the strict orthodoxy of the Flinker family and the secularised position of Yitskhok Rudashevski, who was largely untouched by religious stirrings. Between these two extremes were the somewhat traditional Frank family, and the Racz-Heyman family.

The Heyman-Racz family lived a fairly assimilated lifestyle, some members of the extended family having `married out'. Eva's forebears had embraced conservative-progressive (Neolog) Judaism; her great-grandfather being the first progressive rabbi of Nagyvarad..

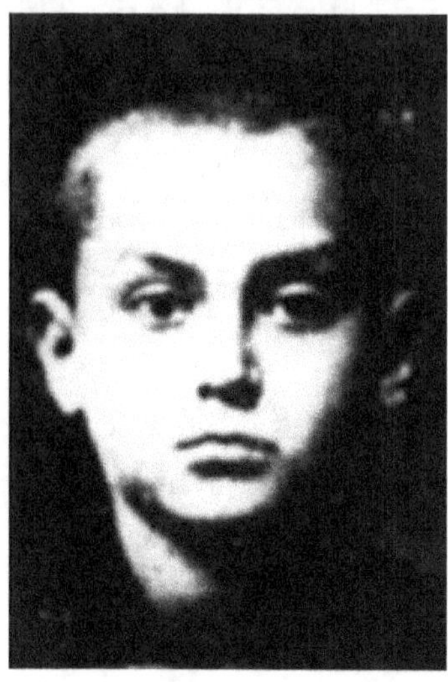

Plate 4.2. Yitskhok Rudashevski.

Public domain.

Politically the four families ranged from the Flinker's staunch conservatism, strongly Zionistic in Moshe's case, to the socialistic leanings of Eva's mother and step-father, and on to the communist convictions of Rudashevski. Four different political perspective are represented. The Franks were liberal-conservatives. Moshe was a religious Zionist, the Heymans were left-wing socialists while Yitskhok was an ardent communist.

In fact the four diaries are representative of many diverse aspects of the religious and political spectrum of which European Jewry, during the period, was composed. There is a unity between the writers, in the midst of such diversity. There is a unity of racial identity, their designation as ‘inferior’, and in the persecutions they bore. Jewish racial identity overshadows the lives of all of these young writers, and is accepted by them as the natural context of life.

Both of the boys' diaries, written in the Jewish languages of Hebrew and Yiddish, were contemporaneous with Anne Frank's but both were terminated during 1943, before Eva Heyman had even commenced to write. Anne's period of writing overlapped with each of them, to some degree.

One date, Dec 7, 1942, is significant in three of these diaries. On this day, which was the fifth day of Hanukkah 5703, both Moshe's and Anne's families lit candles, while Yitskhok Rudashevski attended a club party. Each of these three young diarists, scattered throughout Europe, recorded their celebrations on that day.

Eva and Moshe wrote for relatively short periods of time, three and a half and ten months respectively. During such brief periods maturational change would be less marked, though probably discernible, given the momentous life-style changes these young people endured. Conversely Anne and Yitskhok both wrote between the ages of thirteen and fifteen, and over approximately a two year period. We can, therefore, expect to find evidence of their psychological and social development, as they progressed through adolescence. This is a discernible feature of Yitskhok's diary, and is certainly clearly obvious in Anne's case.

Common elements abound. All four diarists lived lives that were restricted and curtailed by Nazi dominance, with loss of privileges, freedom, wealth and educational opportunities. Each had time to reflect and ponder upon major issues, and to a degree, each attempted to gain an abstract and philosophical understanding of the momentous events in which they had unwillingly become enmeshed. Each diarist struggled with issues of maturity and family relationships, with self-identity, and, most significantly, with preserving their own emotional balance and mental health. Each lived with the spectre of fear for long periods, and, at times, with stark terror. Each identified consciously with the kinship of the Jewish people and all were touched by the suffering of others.

Each identified with the Jewish people, as the ever present context of their newly restricted lives, and with the Jewish religion, whatever their individual religious position. Each benefited, during confinement, from educational pursuits; and each clung to hope to the end.

It has been said, by those close to each of our diarists, that they were particularly emotional and sensitive young people. From the vantage point of history they certainly appear to have been intelligent, keenly observant of human kind and self-analytic.

In her introduction to the Hungarian edition of Eva's diary, her mother Agnes Zsolt (Agi) described Eva as an exceptionally intelligent and sensitive girl, while Yitskhok's friend and fellow student Shoshana Stolitski described him as a very studious student, outstanding in his studies, intelligent, one who took great pains to broaden his knowledge, and an avid reader.

Much of our young diarists' writings are undated - generalised collections, which included historical background material, poetry, speeches, odes and religious material such as prayers and liturgies. This material expands our understanding of the writer's personality, interests, lifestyles and activities and forms a valid part of each diary.

# Chapter 5

Secrecy and Intention

These four diarists wrote with marked intention. For Eva and Anne, who began immediately after their thirteenth birthdays, diary writing was both a sign of maturity and an outlet for their most personal thoughts. Each girl, in fact, personified her diary and wrote to the diary as to an alter-ego. Anne called her diary "Kitty"; while Eva wrote "Dear Diary", in such examples as "Dear Diary, I am taking you along to Aniko's house. Don't worry you wont be alone; you're my best friend"(page 69). Eva, like Anne, wrote to her diary as though it had a separate identity.

While conducting a formal study of the history of the Ghetto, on 5th November, 1942, Yitskhok wrote "I consider that everything should be recorded and noted down, even the most gory, because everything will be taken into account"(p. 84).

Moshe Flinker was aware that they were living in an important age but recorded it all out of a need to keep himself busy and to give his days some structure. "In this manner", he wrote in his first entry "I shall be able to account for all I have done each day" (p. 23). Nine months later he was aware that the purpose of his diary had changed, having become a reflection of his spiritual life, as he grappled with the major issues of faith amidst such suffering.

All writers were exceptionally passionate and possessive about their diaries, which accompanied them into every hide-out or change of dwelling. When Anne's diary was under threat, as a potential risk to household security, Anne was adamant: "Not my diary, if my diary goes, I go with it" (171).

Each diary was discovered, or perhaps more accurately uncovered, by surviving family members, after each writer was deported. The discoverers each had prior knowledge of the diaries existence but no intimate acquaintance with the content. In fact it is almost certain that, prior to the deaths of the diarists, no second persons had been privy to their contents; although all are now read throughout the world. Even though, in a moment of intimacy, Anne Frank had offered to permit her sister, Margot, to read some parts of her diary, and although some parts may have been divulged to Peter Van Daan, there is no indication, or record, of this having taken place.

Secrecy was vital to the intimacy and the verity of the written revelations. All the diarists needed the security of privacy because much that they wrote was critical of others, or highly embarrassing to themselves.

From the first day, her thirteenth birthday, Anne intended to confide in her diary completely "as I have never been able to do in any one before"(p. 12). Similarly Eva's first entry on 13/2/44 contained this entry "Dear Diary, from now on I will carry on this chain the key with which I will lock you so that no one will ever know my secrets" (p. 28). After confiding Agi's socialist ideology to her diary, Eva wrote: "I don't tell these things to anyone but you, dear diary, not to another soul" (55).

Sore Voloshin, Yitskhok's cousin, who rescued his writings long after his deportation, said, "Not once did we discuss his folder of notes with him. He kept it a secret." (10) "He carried it everywhere with him, always hid it. He showed it to no one. So important, so dear was it to him" (148). Though they were less ritualistic in their deliberate secrecy than were the girls, the boys were no less committed to their privacy. Towards the end of his diary, Yitskhok, a devoted supported of the Red Army to the end, began to use a code, such as 'P' for Pioneer and initials for the names of fellow admirers of the Red Army, apparently aware of the danger that this material might fall into Nazi hands.

Moshe commented intimately about his parent's relationship in a manner which teenagers in any culture are not usually permitted to do. A degree of assurance of secrecy is certainly indicated by the fact that he felt the freedom to write in this way.

The diarists discerned the importance of their experiences and were profoundly effected both mentally and emotionally, but being immature, felt the need for their mental and emotional turmoil to remain hidden. Hence Anne's offer to Margot was a sign of trust and openness. Had she followed through with the offer it would have been a partial unveiling of her real Self. Each diarist also sensed a need for increased privacy in the crowded conditions of their confinement. Anne in particular, the most restricted of the four, felt the pain of being deprived of privacy.

For the boys, who did not personify their diaries, and wrote in notebooks and on scrap papers, rather than in formal `diaries', the need for secrecy was less self-conscious, but it obviously existed, given the personally and politically sensitive nature of the contents.

Anne and Moshe began their diaries systematically with a précis of their family origins, while Eva, nonchalantly and with naiveté, referred to her family background and early life in passing. Yitskhok appears to have made a number of attempts to launch into his writing, as though, at first, systematic application to the task was difficult for him.

Yitskhok's entries prior to 12/9/'42 are only erratically dated and read as a summary of events. For this early material he used general sub-headings. For example one entry is made under the sub-heading "the first ghetto days speed by"(34) and another reads: "It is the end of the summer of 1941"(30). This material provides the background to his life in the Vilna Ghetto before he commenced his later and more systematic daily reporting.

# Chapter 6

## The Four Families

Each of the four young diarists entered the period of their confinement living more or less comfortably within a nuclear family circle. This comfort underwent rapid decline, due to the reality of life under Fascist rule. Forces beyond their control made the young people, and their parents, the victims of social upheaval, which resulted in major changes in family dynamics.

A necessary change in location was the first force to impinge upon their lives. Anne's family, which had moved from Germany to escape the Nazi threat, before Anne started school, was forced into hiding, along with four non-family members, Mr & Mrs Van Daan and their son Peter, and later, Mr Dussel. Moshe's family of seven children, with their parents, transferred from Holland to various dwellings in Brussels, Belgium.

Yitskhok's family were first ghettoised and subsequently forcibly relocated to different dwellings. They often fled into malines, or secret hide-outs, as the Vilna Ghetto was progressively liquidated.

The Flinker family chose to escape from Holland to Belgium because few people knew them there. Having reached Brussels with the family intact they attempted to pass as Arians.

Eva Heyman's situation was somewhat different from the other three, who lived with both of their parents. Because Eva's parents had separated when Eva was four years old, she lived, not with her mother and step-father, Agi and Bela Zsolt, who resided in Budapest, but with her maternal grand-parents, Mr and Mrs Racz. The Racz extended family circle appears to have actually included Eva's Aryan governess Juszti, and the devoted family servant, Mariska. Eva's biological father and paternal grandmother lived nearby, also in Nagyvarad.

Step-father Bela Zsolt's dismissal from his newspaper confined him and Agi, Eva's mother, to 'Varad, where they remained until their escape with false papers shortly after Eva's last diary entry was written. Their presence in the home pleased Eva greatly, so much so that she wrote "It's so different with the Agis at home that I don't even care if the war goes on for a long time"(47).

After Kristallnacht the Frank family escaped from Frankfurt to Holland, although they obviously did not escape far enough. Before the surrender of the Netherlands to Germany, on 15th May, 1940, Anne had lived in Amsterdam with her parents and older sister Margot.

Moshe was born in The Hague, Holland, of Polish born parents. He was the oldest son, having an older sister, four younger sisters and infant brother, nine people in all. In contrast, in distant Vilna, Yitskhok Rudashevski's household was composed of his parents, his grandmother and himself.

Each of the families were people of education, culture and considerable financial means. For example, despite his large family Moshe's father, Eliezer Flinker, managed to pay large bribes to obtain residential permits, and fed his family out of savings and investments. Eva's grandfather, Mr Racz, owned a prosperous pharmacy. Her father, Bela Heyman, was an architect, and her step-father, Bela Zsolt, a noted newspaper journalist.

Prior to the German invasion of Eastern Poland, Elihu Rudashevski was a typesetter for a Yiddish Newspaper and his wife, Rose, was a skilled seamstress. They were comparatively comfortable and remained so in the Vilna Ghetto.

Otto Frank had been managing director of a firm called Travies NV in Holland, which also employed Mr Van Daan, fellow occupant of the Secret Annexe. Anne's grandparents were all wealthy and, in fact, Anne commented once that she and Margot were granddaughters of a millionaire.

Each family was either interned in a ghetto, or fled from their former place of residence. The loss of home and possessions left a wistfulness and soft sense of loss in the young people, but the loss of possessions was far less damaging to the four youngsters than either the threat of future loss or the actual loss of significant others. Anne expressed it this way: "Memories mean more to me than dresses" (23). Anne demonstrated this by taking into hiding: first her diary, then hair curlers, school books, a comb and old letters. She took only one summer dress, which became a source of difficulty, especially as she was at the stage of rapid adolescent growth (5 and 23).

Early in her diary Anne wrote of her deceased maternal grandmother, who had lived with them for about four years: "no one will ever know how much

she is present in my thoughts and how much I love her still"(15).

How much more painful than the loss of home and possessions was the arrest and removal of loved ones for probable slaughter. Eva, for example, was very perturbed by the realisation, after her father, Bela Heyman, was imprisoned as a hostage, that Grandpa Racz could also be imprisoned. Eva carried his daily supply of food to him, a task which the children managed to accomplish more successfully than the adults. Eva's fear was exacerbated by Agi's terror that her husband, Uncle Bela, risked arrest for being a `fighting socialist'.

During an early deportation from Vilna Ghetto, Yitskhok's grandmother was forcibly and finally separated from the younger and stronger family members. The thirteen year old boy did not write extensively about this tragedy but others testify that he felt her loss keenly, and he did chronicle: "Grandmother cannot go with us. We are in despair....We quickly say good-by to grandmother: - for ever. We leave her alone in the middle of the street and run to save ourselves. I shall never forget the two imploring hands and eyes which begged :"`Take me along!' We left the ghetto... Mother is cry-ing. We cannot forget that we have abandoned grandmother" (pp. 44-45).

One of Eva's greatest losses occurred when Juszti, her governess and `substitute mother', had to leave the home, as her employment in a Jewish household was forbidden. This was before Eva's diary was begun, but Juszti was not permanently missing. She continued to visit the family, as did Mariska their former cook, who kept Eva's diary safe until Eva's mother returned after the war.

Eva was particularly distressed by the loss of her dear friend Marta Munzer, whom she knew had been killed. The memory of Marta's last hours with her and of their two red bicycles standing side by side at the gate was a constant and oppressive shadow, which reminded Eva of her own impending fate. It is not without significance that Eva wrote about Marta Munzer in her first and her last diary entries, as well as on intermediary dates. Marta was her constant pre-occupation. Agi later related that uncontrollable bouts of distress accompanied these memories, while Eva, for her part, recorded: "Agi cried a lot whenever she saw the two red bicycles standing along side each other" (32). Their distress was obviously mutual, and each exacerbated the other.

Yitskhok Rudashevski's extended family actually expanded during ghettoization, as the wider family formed stronger links, co-operated together and tried to support each other. When the boy became temporarily separated from his parents he took refuge in a hideout with his uncles and cousins, who included Sore Voloshin, the girl who rescued his diary on 13/7/44. Later his cousins, when separated from their father, survived by being registered on the Rudashevski's yellow work certificate.

On the 25th October, 1942, Yitskhok recorded that his uncle's family shared one room with his own - seven people in all. In the ghetto Uncle's tragedies became his own tragedies and on 28th December, 1942 he described the seizure of 800 roubles from his uncle probably the last money he had. "Uncles troubles settled so heavily on my spirit"; he wrote (114).

Once safely in Brussels, the Flinker family were discrete, kept a low profile, rarely went outdoors and kept to themselves; so much so that at one point Moshe lamented "I am in touch with no one"(88). The family drifted towards mixing with other Jewish people and Moshe recorded meetings with the Rabbi and visits to the Jewish library (while it was still operational). They socialised with other Jews, the ritual slaughterer, the beadle, the Kosher butcher, and a Hebrew teacher who had been a friend in Holland.

Once their residential status seemed secure they became bolder. In about April of 1943 Moshe enrolled in a school of secretarial studies where he met new friends, gentiles, both admirable youths, and others whose lifestyle was so distant that he accorded them little respect.

Moshe's most painful feelings of loss centred on his separation from his beloved land, Israel, and on his Jewish brethren, those unknown multitudes who were suffering in the east; as were those whom he personally knew. Moshe wrote: "My people and my country do not leave my thoughts for even a moment; all day long they are in my mind. Several times already I have asked myself whether I will ever get the chance to stand on its holy earth if the Lord will ever permit me to walk about my land"(82).

Moshe's pain also embraced former teachers and friends whose fate profoundly disturbed him, especially his friend Finkel and a certain girl in The Hague. On April 7, 1943 he wrote: "During recent days I have been gripped by terrible sensations of loneliness, isolation and dejection. I believe that the reasons for this are that I so often think about my people - from which I am far removed - and the tragic image of the girl in The Hague crosses my mind so frequently. I also suffer from the fact that there is no one here to whom I might talk and expect to be heard with understanding" (82).

# Chapter 7

———

## Within the Family

Initially Eva spent some time in her diary discussing the questions of her mother's love for her and the issue of her mother's comparative love for others. This was an issue of major importance to Eva, and in the light of Eva's placement with her grandparents, after her mother married Bela Zsolt, it is not surprising that it surfaced in the first paragraph of the first entry in her diary.

Juszti's letter to Agi of 21/11/1945, in which she admonishes Agi (and herself) for not having tried harder to save Eva, supports that Eva's perceptions may have been justified, however the fact that the Zsolts returned from France (and possible escape) because Agi missed Eva so much, suggests that Eva was mistaken. The fact that the false papers, which facilitated the Zsolt's escape did not include Eva is not conclusive evidence of her mother's lack of love, because previously, in April, 1944, false stolen papers for all three were obtained for Agi by a Christian cousin. That earlier provision had been declined by Agi because of her own mother's hysterical distress at the mention of their departure.

Although it is probable that her husband was indeed Agi's greatest love, this is usual, and normally not of concern their children. Eva's preoccupation with the "scale of priorities" in Agi's heart and her lack of confidence in her family relations, reflects, not only that she was the child of divorced parents and was unhappy not to be living in Budapest with her mother, but that she had once overheard the adults saying that she had an "unhappy childhood".

Eva, for her part, reserved her deepest affections for Juszti who, by Nazi decree had to be employed elsewhere, although she often visited, and helped out. After five days of confinement in the ghetto Eva wrote: "At night I dreamt about Juszti dear diary and in the morning I woke up crying" (92). Initially, however, on 5/5/1944, the day after her confinement, she had written: "Strange as it seems, everybody belonging to us was here together with us, everybody in the world whom we loved"(88-89). Juszti was something of an outsider, yet she was truly the object of Eva's most significant love. It seems that, because Juszti was not a family member, Eva momentarily overlooked her, although previously she had written: "I love Juszti more than anyone else in the world, a little more than Agi but right after her"(36).

Much later, when separated from her father, with whom she had not shared a home for nine years Eva wrote: "I had begun to miss my father very much" (95). Eva, who commenced her diary agonising over her mother's love, found that her need for contact with all her loved ones increased as the threat of separation became greater.

It appears that Yitskhok was close to his parents, watchful of their needs and dutiful, meeting them at the Ghetto gate after work, doing housework and cooking, staying home from school when his mother was ill, caring for her needs, and sometimes accompanying his father to work. His mother shared some aspects of her daily life outside the Ghetto with him but his real preoccupation was with youth activities and school friends. His idols were not members of his family, but his teachers. After they were confined to the ghetto the need to work and to obtain protected-workers' certificates dominated his parents actions. Yitskhok helped them bear these burdens by behaving cooperatively and being domesticated, but it does appear that his emotional needs were somewhat unmet. He came increasingly to seek friendship and camaraderie from ghetto cultural circles and educational activities and spent increasing amounts of time with these companions.

Although Yitskhok does not speak of his own loneliness he shows the finely tuned and sensitive understanding of other's pain and loss which, in one so youthful, only comes from suffering, experienced first hand. Upon the death of Dr. Moshe Heller on 7/11/1942 he wrote of his friend Gabik Heller: "I feel great pity for Gabik, for his mother. How terrible is the lot of these quiet, lonely people. How honestly, how poorly did they live, how quiet and refined they were! How hard will it be now for Gabik, how he loved his father! Gabik's misfortune struck deep into my heart" (88).

The Flinker nuclear family of nine people remained intact but became somewhat enmeshed and conflicted during their time in Brussels. At first they were under virtual self-imposed house confinement, due to Mr Flinker's fear of disclosure if he sought employment. Later Moshe became engaged in formal education and was able to distance himself somewhat from the marital conflict which dominated the family's interactions.

Mrs Flinker's desire to attempt a further escape, her frustration with her husband's unemployment, the need to keep the children indoors during school hours, the children's quarrels and the almost continuous stress of their tenuous residential status resulted in repeated quarrels, and outbursts of tearful distress on her part. She was often agitated and distressed, for example on 2/1/1943 Moshe wrote: "my mother is very sad. Every other moment she cries. At night she is afraid to go to sleep for fear the Germans will come and take her, because their custom is to come at night"(75).

Moshe's own inner turmoil and existential anguish does not appear to have been understood by his family. He frequently felt sorrow and anguish at heart, and occasionally expressed extremes of loneliness. On March 9, 1943 he had penned this statement: "Lately I feel so lonely, so barren - a feeling I have never had before"(81). When thinking back to his days in The Hague, days in which he believed himself to have been self-contained, Moshe wrote "In those days I used to say that if, at rare intervals, I should ever feel the need to pour out my heart I would pour it out to myself. But from then until now I find myself completely changed. I didn't know then what it was to live without knowing anyone even a little, without having anyone, to be as lonely as if one were in a desert"(83).

As the oldest son, Moshe's father took an extra interest in his education and his religious training. Occasionally he confided with Moshe on a personal basis, for example it was Mr Flinker who first disclosed to Moshe, in December, 1942, that one hundred thousand Jews had already been killed in the east. Moshe appears to have later engaged in denial or repression of the information; although the extremes of anguish that he felt demonstrate that he really did comprehend the implications of his father's disclosure. Moshe did not perceive this significant conversation with his father as a shared confidence, but felt resentful, as though his father had only told him in order to rub salt into his wounds.

While Mr Flinker attempted to assist Moshe's religious education and reading, their relationship was sometimes strained by differences of opinion about such matters as the course of the war, and the desirability of an Allied victory. Moshe's attitude to his father was rather complex. He was distressed at his parents' quarrels, their trading of insults and his mother's continuous nagging. He developed a burning resentment for the matchmakers who deal in love "as people do with merchandise" and who regard a marriage as merely a business transaction. His parents union, as Polish born Jews, had obviously been organised by their ilk. While Moshe submitted to his father's wishes on matters of education, but his sympathies appear to have been with his mother, who had bad dreams and often cried.

Moshe, like Anne, was irked by the restrictions his parents imposed. He felt hemmed in on all sides, like a caged bird, and he described his parents as having excessive watchfulness which inhibited his every act and accomplishment. Anne's family, like Moshe's, was in close physical proximity; yet the very closeness necessitated a distancing of themselves, and emotional isolation which prevented the adult family members from being able to satisfy the three teenagers' need for love and emotional support. Perhaps the most poignant statement Anne made, which summarised the needs of each of these adolescents, was, "I simply long for a word of comfort, for someone who could give sound advice and also draw out some of my real self; but, alas, I keep on looking, but I haven't found anyone yet" (207).

In general all of the adults were themselves experiencing the same, or more harrowing fears, such as responsibility for feeding the family and the constant awareness of external threats, so they were increasingly unable to meet the needs of the young.

Marital conflict does not appear to have been a major reaction to confinement in the Frank family but there was an extreme degree of interpersonal conflicts within the wider household. For two years, two nuclear families, the Franks and the Van Daans, along with Mr Dussel, were confined together in very close quarters. Marital conflict between Mr & Mrs Van Daan erupted periodically and this increased the tension in the whole household. Much conflict between the various adults and family groupings occurred and there was considerable ` scape-goating' of poor Anne, who was the youngest household member. Anne was also the most immature, the most emotionally vulnerable and most physically active of the three young people in the Secret Annexe. After sixteen months in hiding, Anne, in exasperation, had written: "Alone I had to face the difficult task of changing myself, to stop the everlasting reproaches, which were so oppressive and which reduced me to such terrible despondency" (145).

The conflict, and the criticism of everything Anne said and did, were exacerbated by the secrecy and restrictions within which they were forced to live. (Even gazing at the sky through an open window had its risks.) Anne's list of failings were often brought out into the open, and fully ventilated by her critics. She was the identified miscreant in the household, rebuked, abused and accused by everyone. This created a gap between herself and members of her family. Anne's mother was incapable of fathoming the cause of her pain, rage and tears, and she was only partially understood by her father.

Anne's problems meant that Margot and Peter had to distance themselves from her, in order to appear more mature, and more closely allied with the adults, in order not to be placed in the same negative light.

Anne reported that Mrs Frank's behaviours towards her included tactlessness, crude jokes and hard words, but it was Anne's perception that her mother pushed her away and was unable to love her, and understand her, that maximised the emotional distance between them. Anne responded to this perception by refusing overtures of mother-daughter intimacy and, in the early months, by openly coveting her father's affections.

In response to the pain of rejection, Anne wrote a certain unfortunate and critical letter to her father. Mr Frank, who was nicknamed Pym, responded with deep hurt. This widened the gap between himself and Anne and further alienated her at a time when she beginning to mature out of her childish impulsiveness and could have expected more acceptance in the household. Following this incident, on 15/7/1944, she wrote: "I concealed from Daddy everything that perturbed me; I never shared my ideals with him. I was aware of the fact that I was pushing him away from me ...... This is a point I think a lot about: Why is it that Pym annoys me? so much so that I can hardly bear him teaching me, that his affectionate ways strike me as being put on, that I want to be left in peace and would really prefer it if he dropped me a bit, until I felt more certain in my attitude towards him?" (217).

A major cause for this change of heart was the guilt which Anne experienced after writing that critical letter. It increased the emotional distance between father and daughter, at a time when Anne's relations with her mother were improving, so, in hindsight perhaps, the unfortunate letter enabled Anne to undergo a more balanced and independent emotional development. In general Anne experienced much upheaval and heart searching about her relations with her parents. She varied from spurning her mother, to tolerating her despite her evident weaknesses. She oscillated from heavy dependence on her father, to a need for emotional space from them all; a need for room to grow up.

Anne, like Moshe, expressed deep loneliness. Shortly before the end, on 15th July, 1944, she wrote: "I felt so frightfully lonely for a long time so left out, neglected and misunderstood" (216). As a response to her mother's rejection, Anne came to believe that she had outgrown the need for her mother. Anne accurately described the emotional barrier she deliberately created, when she admonished herself that she must not overdo her indifference towards her mother. Early in her writings Anne appeared to idolise her father.

The late inclusion of Mr Dussel in the household of the Secret Annexe had many negative consequences for Anne and widened the gap between her and Margot, who was moved out of their shared bedroom. Mr Dussel excluded Anne from the privacy of her room for many hours of each day and he proved to be yet another person with reason to criticise her. His presence created a third force in every inter-family or inter-personal conflict.

This highly pressurised household atmosphere was relieved only by their gentile protectors, who came to visit from outside, Mr Kraler, Mr Koophuis, Elli, Miep and her husband Hank. They brought food, news from the outside world and a little laughter, which temporarily reduced the tension in the strained household. Anne once said that what she needed was some rollicking fun. Those visits from the outside, especially for special occasions, like St Nicholas Day and birthdays, were the nearest Anne came to fun.

# Chapter 8

Friendship and Love

Anne's most intriguing relationship was with 'Petel', as she called Peter Wessel. He was an almost forgotten romantic figure from her past, who influenced her in much the same way as Pista Vadas influenced Eva Heyman, after each boy appeared in the girls' respective dreams.

Anne's heightened romantic longings for her idealised Peter came to be projected onto fellow occupant of the Secret Annexe, Peter Van Daan, so that the two became as one. This was a confusion of identity that Anne, herself, admitted to. This mixture of love-romance and idealisation was not harmful, on the contrary, as a powerful and positive force, it assisted her psychological growth. Out of the love and enveloping warmth that the dream provided, Anne became more optimistic and more understanding in her attitude to the Van Daans, and freer to grow to love (the ordinary) Peter. It strengthened her to withstand the conflicts, yells, screams, disagreements, stamping and abuse (95) and the criticism from others, so that she was able to write: "You can't and mustn't regard me as fourteen, for these troubles have made me older"(188).

Because much of the household venom in the Secret Annex was directed towards Anne, she replaced intimacy with her parents, not with the self-containment she believed she had acquired, but with a some-what improved relationship with her sister Margot and the warmth and acceptance provided by her romance with Peter Van Daan. Anne admitted this, when, on 28/4/1944 she wrote: "I have longed so much and for so long-I am so lonely-now I have found consolation"(183).

Yet the years Anne had endured in hiding, and the insights into human behaviour she had so painfully acquired, prevented her from surrendering naively to the natural attractions which this romance offered. She was able to maintain the balance between meeting her own needs for affection, the emotional and physical restrictions within the household, and Peter's own emotional and intellectual limitations. As the romance progressed Anne became aware of the poor fit between Peter's personality and her own expectations, desires, hopes and needs. She was disappointed in Peter in a number of ways: his disdain for religion, lack of will power, life goals, independence, character and self-esteem. Five months after the romance began Anne wrote. "He is beginning to lean on me a bit and that musn't happen under any circumstances. A type like Peter finds it difficult to stand on his own feet" (212) and also "He has no religion, scoffs at Jesus Christ, and swears using the Name of God; although I'm not Orthodox either, it hurts me every time I see how deserted, how scornful and how poor he really is" (212).

Eva, at thirteen, like Anne, had begun to have an interest in the opposite sex, for which her grandmother often scolded her, claiming that boys were the only thing that Eva had on her mind and that it was shameless to run after them. Despite these admonitions, on 26/2/44 Eva recorded in her diary: "Dear Diary, something very odd has happened to me. I almost don't have the courage to confess it to you. I think I'm in love. I'm even writing his name down: Pista Vadas" (40).

Pista Vadas, unlike Peter Van Daan, was already a mature young man, and he thought of Eva as "just a little girl". Romance didn't develop between them but Pista was friendly and encouraging to Eva and helpful and attentive towards her family in the ghetto. His friendly presence was a comfort, and Eva confided some of her fears to him, and shared strawberries with him. Following Agi's example he called her "Eva-Doll" which made her conclude: "Now I see ..... that he likes me after all" (99).

Yitskhok, although an only child, was not a social isolate. He formed many relationships with adults, mainly teachers and leaders in the ghetto clubs. His real idols were his teachers, such as teacher Gershteyn, and especially his mentor and fellow socialist Mire Bernshteyn. While he had many friends, like Gabik, Benke Nayer, Serke and Mulke Lurie they were his comrades and really did not share the intimacy of his interior life. They shared his co-operative ventures in school, "Young Pioneers", and youth organisation activities. Yitskhok was a very goal-centred boy, who showed no indication of a romantic attachment to any particular girl, although he worked closely with girls on many projects.

Moshe regarded contact between the sexes as a matter of "Holy seriousness", which was outside the range of his experience. Previously, however, in The Hague, he had found himself strongly attracted to a young Jewish girl. He stated that he had loved her and continued to love her. He wrote "She almost never spoke to me, nor did I speak to her, never the less, I still feel that I could recognise her glances of love towards me" (56). Moshe's reverie centred upon this girl, and former friendships yet in his confined circumstances in Brussels, he began to long for friendship.

Seeing the shallowness of the local students of both sexes, he turned from them, back to longing for his previous friend, Finkel. Later, almost despite himself he began, tenuously, to form friendships with local gentile lads. He became so close to one unnamed friend (possibly Roger) that he was tempted to reveal his Jewish racial identity before this friend departed for England. The caution which life "incognito" had instilled in him, however, caused Moshe to hold back and to think only that some day, after the war, they would be able to meet again, possibly on equal terms or perhaps with the Jewish people in the more honourable or exalted position.

Finally, in virtually the last entry in his diary, Moshe related that a new and significant friend, twenty one year old fellow student Marcel Dutrange, had entered his life and had become a positive influence upon him. This friendship obviously contained within it the possibility of some compensation for the void created in Moshe's life by the stress and extremis under which he lived. The termination of Moshe's diary means that information about the course of this valuable relationship will remain a mystery. What we do know is that this friendship changed Moshe completely. "He has influenced me so much" Moshe wrote, "that I am amazed when I think about it."(115). Given the loneliness and sorrow that Moshe experienced, change was something he needed.

# Chapter 9

Gentiles, Great Contradiction

Each family had positive, even intimate connections with Christians. Some close relatives, such as Eva's own father, Bela Heyman, had converted. Others had married out, like Bela Hayman's sister, Eva's Aunt Lili, a woman who, never-the-less, voluntarily entered the Ghetto with her mother, and died.

Some Christians, such as the office staff at the Secret Annexe, were their protectors. Some provided temporary shelter, like the factory owner who housed the Flinkers when they first reached Brussels. Others stole documents to facilitate their escape, while still others helped in less dangerous ways. Examples of this latter help were the three Bishops who wrote letters of reference for Mr Racz in support of the return of his pharmacy. Still others provided sympathy; or perhaps, at great cost to themselves in such difficult days, a little food.

Yitskhok recorded his discovery of the true racial identity of a ragged boy who lived as a gentile with a local farmer when they two brought a cart load of meat into the ghetto: but he made no wonderment of the farmer's daring. Yitskhok also recorded the entry of gentiles into the ghetto:"Gentiles are standing and taking part in our sorrow. Some Jews hire gentile boys to help carry the bundles." Later he described how a German women gave his mother soap, flour, pieces of candy and bread saying: "The war will end, the Fuhrer is to blame for everything, you will be liberated, they need you, you are useful industrious people. We Germans and you Jews will not suffer long!" (81).

Eva's family contacts and marriage connections with gentiles were numerous, and people of many political and religious persuasions visited the home, even after the Germany invaders had forbidden social contact with Jews.

Eva noted the reactions of the city's Archives Director, Zoltan Nadanyi, who visited Agi and Uncle Bela every evening. "Altogether Uncle Zoltan is sad, just as if he werte a Jew, and he is a read Aryan!" (77).

Chief among those who helped Eva were Mariska, Juszti. Agi's Christian cousin stole papers from his work place in an unsuccessful attempt to facilitate their escape, while Mrs Jacobi, their dressmaker, offered to conceal Eva. Both of these offers were declined, because of Grandmother Racz' irrational mental state, and the hysterical tears with which the rescue plans were greeted. Juszti obtained approval from her new employer, Mrs Poroszlay, to conceal Eva on their farm, but her husband's adamant refusal to agree thwarted yet another gentile attempt to rescue Eva.

Moshe wrote a short undated entry about a friend, Roger, whom he wished well when their paths separated. This was possibly the same gentile friend who went to England, who invited him for holiday in the Ardennes, and whose parents had provided lodgings when Moshe first arrived in Brussels.

Gentiles helped each of the diarists, and there is no reflection of any anti-Aryan hostility in their writings. Anne in particular, developed a warm love for her protectors, and a special affinity with the young women, Miep and Elli, who confided in her as with an adult.

Here-in lies one of the mysteries of the Shoah. For every Aryan who helped them thousands made their lot worse, but no one has ever been able to adequately account for why some were ʻrighteous gentiles', while some only risked their lives to save Jews for the money they were paid, and yet others were their persecutors.

Numerous reasons have been given for their actions by the `righteous from the nations', a wide assortment of motives; some of which are as vague as "it seemed the logical thing to do" and "I thought it was what everyone would do in such circumstances".

One of the more unfathomable mysteries of the Shoah is, however, how ordinary people, loving family members, from civilized, Christian nations, could become so barbaric, so quickly and so easily.

This is the mystery which led Eva, to whom the Christians, Juszti and Mariska, were so dear, to write bitterly: "If the Aryans had wanted to they could have prevented our being put in the Ghetto. But they are glad about it, and now they don't care what happens to us" (104).

# Chapter 10

Severity of Stress

Each of the following are sources of distress, are known to cause stress reactions, irrespective of an individual's physical or emotional history. The stronger these forces operate, the greater the degree of stress.

a) change to the person's life

b) loss of control over ones own life

c) the perceived undesirability of the change

d) the number of stress factors impinging simultaneously.

Each of the four diarists families experienced stress from odious Nazi demands, with major loss of control over their own lives. Place of residence, schooling, and social status were changed against their will. Each family was assaulted by multiple fears, such as fear of arrest and fear of death, and had prolonged stress from a number of different sources: property confiscation, financial insecurity, poor living conditions, food shortages, health problems, and the loss or arrest of numerous family members or friends. Such stress, if it extends for over six months, is known to predispose children and adults to mental illness. Each diarist, except Eva, experienced long, rather than shorter periods of stress. Some of the adults, such as Mrs Van Daan and Grandpa Racz, spoke about suicide but these young people maintained positive mental outlooks. The mental health of the four diarists and their positive attitudes, are a credit to them.

# Chapter 11

Family and Household Relations

THE FLINKER FAMILY experienced much stress from marital and familial relationships, although discord with non-family members was minimal. The inability of the seven children to attend school, and Mr Flinker's unemployment were major causes of stress for Mrs Flinker. Their immigration to Belgium and the frequent and major changes in their accommodation caused them to worry and there were frequent crises with regard to their financial security because of their dependence on the value of shares purchased in Holland. Legal problems surrounding identity papers and their 'Aryan' status, were intermittent but critical threats which could have led to their discovery. The threat of arrest was always present.

The Rudashevski family experienced little marital and familial stress. Inter-personal relationships were relatively stress free but the loss of their grandmother was a major sorrow. Unemployment worries were continual, for both of Yitskhok's parents; and their living circumstances underwent almost continuous upheaval. Financial doom was an ever present threat. The need to obtain the documentation and the legal status to avoid being deported were virtually continuous in the Ghetto, and the struggle to obtain food was continual. Man-made disasters and persecutions were by far the greatest source of anxiety, even terror, in the Vilna Ghetto.

In the Frank family's case there was little marital but much familial conflict. The major problems emanated from inter-personal relations. Unemployment and non-school attendance, drastic changes in living circumstances, some financial disability, the fear of legal problems such as arrest and imprisonment, and stress from such man-made factors included bombings, food shortages, police inspections and threats to their protectors' safety. Anne's emerging independence and the changes of adolescence formed the background to her entire period in hiding.

In the Heyman-Racz household conjugal conflict was minimal because Mr Racz was forbearing and always gave in to his wife. This was a strategy which worked until Grandma Racz became irrational, with the breakdown of her mental health. Previous family conflicts were then exacerbated. Gradually friends and neighbours were taken, and Grandpa Racz was forced out of his pharmacy for the second time. This resulted in financial difficulties, as the family had to borrow money to live. The Racz family suffered the same fear of impending arrest and deportation as the Frank family, as well as the stress of food shortages and persecutions. Mr Racz' illness, Agi's slow recovery from an operation and Mrs Racz' mental health meant that health problems were serious. This made the family very dependent upon Juszti who sneaked in frequently to help out. Ghettoisation made a major and catastrophic changes to their living circumstances, crowding many together and depriving them of all their treasured and valuable worldly belongings. When compared with the other diarists, Eva's family's experience of catastrophe was relatively short lived, but never-the-less was extreme.

# Chapter 12

———

Reactions to Stress

Whilst their writings demonstrate that the emotional needs of the young people often went unmet, every other individual was in similar deep need, and therefore possessed few resources of optimism, strength, comfort and love to carry even their own emotional burdens. Grandpa Racz, for example, was a source of strength to others in his family, yet he was reduced to contemplate suicide. As ghetto pharmacist, he supplied poison from the hospital, to the old people who requested it, and eventually he begged Agi to permit him to suicide too. Although she refused her consent, Agi, who worked in the ghetto hospital, understood the situation. She knew that suicides were so numerous in 'Varad, in mid 1944, that the makeshift mortuary was always filled beyond capacity.

The terrible circumstances led to some mental illness, even though the families tried to conceal the truth, as Eva wrote: "Agi didn't even tell Agi Friedlander, who is her best friend in Varad, what a terrible thing had happened to Grandma, she only said that Grandma's nerves were very bad. It looks like Agi is ashamed that Grandma is out of her mind, even though nobody can be blamed for it except that damned Hitler"(80). Grandma Racz' symptoms included a continual preoccupation with cleaning the silver, until it was all confiscated by the Germans, where upon she repeatedly and compulsively performed the same house-cleaning tasks. Other symptoms were fears, fits of hysterical distress (including screeching, door banging, and eye rolling), wild accusations and tempestuous outbursts, which were subdued only by medication.

The doctor's diagnosis, that she would amend when circumstances improved because she was not actually insane, was borne out when her condition suddenly vanished after the dreaded decision was made and the family was actually confined to the ghetto.

Eva maintained her enthusiasm for life and her warm and positive emotional attachments. Whilst increased irritability was found in other members of the family, she remained cheerful, even though she absorbed some of her mother's terror and extremes of response.

Moshe wrote of Mrs Keller, a woman of goodness and works of charity, who had been deported with her family: "I never before imagined that from the immensity of one's troubles one can go mad, but now I have found that even this affliction has not been spared us. Madness too is among us"(75). Having written this Moshe became aware that he had unconsciously been concerned about his own mother's psychological state, whenever he saw her depressed.

---

## SURVIVOR GUILT

One characteristic response to having survived a natural or man-made catastrophe or serious accident, "survivor guilt", was frequently expressed by the diarists, in particular by Anne, Eva and Moshe. Because Yitskhok's life was not, in any way, one of comfort and because he was so close to danger, frequently within sight of deportations, he did not suffer these guilt feelings.

Anne wrote of her friend, Lies: "I am not more virtuous than she; she, too, wanted to do what was right, why should I be chosen to live and she probably to die? What was the difference between us? (106).

Moshe frequently expressed this same emotion. He felt it so keenly that he contemplated volunteering to join his suffering people. Of his escape to Belgium, where survival was more probable, he wrote: "I see myself as a traitor, who fled from his people at the time of their anguish" (65). He engaged in voluntary privations in sympathy, such as eating only once a day, and forgoing all pleasures and recreations. "I only looked for ways to torture myself. With all my body and soul I wished to be with my people and share their bitter fate. When trouble befalls them so shall it befall me. I wish to be a part of my people. I do not know if I can succeed in chasing the small joys from my heart, but I shall find ways"; he wrote (70).

<u>Fear and Depression</u>

While Yitskhok's describes one fear reaction as "cold fear", on another occasion he wrote: "My heart beats as though with hammers to the cadence of the storm outside. Soon I feel that the storm is approaching us. My head is dizzy, cold perspiration oozes forth, my heart stops beating entirely" (59).

His experiences in hiding must have been events which triggered major fear reactions, but it is Anne's diary which gives us the most frequent and thorough accounts of these experiences, and the short term symptoms they generated. After police raids and burglaries Anne listed trembling, pallor, sweating, palpitations, chattering teeth, knocking knees and extremes of gastro-intestinal disorders as her main reactions to stress.

Moshes' psychological states were, in some respects, the most disquieting. He suffered periods of depression, characterised by lethargy, poor concentration, feelings of emptiness and inner void, worthlessness, numbness and existential anguish. Also he, more than any other, engaged in self-privations and he suffered more distressing `survivor guilt.'

Moshes' dreams, while centring on loved ones, lacked the warmth and comfort which Anne derived from hers.

Because he was subject to prolonged exposure to a stressful situation, and because his depressive states probably persist for the best part of a year his mental state probably hovered on the verge of chronic depression.

## NIGHTMARES

Eva experienced distressing recollections and recurrent nightmares, which generalised into imaginary 'fear dreams' and hallucinatory type experiences during the transition to and from sleep. Eva was distressed by symbols which represented her friend Marta, such as the red bicycle. Her symptoms persisted for an extended time. Her thematic nightmares centred upon the loss of Marta and Juszti. Fears, vivid and detailed recollections of her dreams, and serious feelings of personal threat were present. One especially vivid dream, which, upon awakening, she recounted to her cousin Marica, concerned the method by which Marta died and led Marica to beg her not to talk about her dreams again.

Eva's nightmares, accompanied by screams and crying, were worst when the family pharmacy was first taken from Mr Racz. A possible repetition of this event continued to worry Eva, while awake and asleep, and in the ghetto her

distressing dreams intensified.

Simple nightmares, as opposed to the more complex night terrors, are one of the most common reactions to stress and fear, and each diarist recorded nightmare episodes. Anne wrote: "Why do I always dream and think of the most terrible things - my fear makes me want to scream out loud sometimes" (111). Anne suffered similar dreams to those of Eva. Anne noted the unusual vividness of her dreams in hiding. Recurrent themes were loss and separation, especially from her grandmothers. A particularly distressing theme concerned the fate of her former school fiend, Lies, who first figured in a particularly vivid dream, which was almost a vision. On 27/11/1943 Anne wrote: "Yesterday evening, before I fell asleep, who should suddenly appear before my eyes but Lies! I saw her in front of me, clothed in rags, her face thin and worn. Her eyes were very big and she looked so sadly and reproachfully at me, that I could read in her eyes: "Oh, Anne, why have you deserted me? Help, oh help me, rescue me from this hell!" (105).

Anne's dream material oscillated between the very distressing, and the very comforting. Her dreams of Petel included looking into his velvety brown eyes and hearing him say: "If I had only known I would have come to you long before!" (116), whereas her maternal grandmother, who appeared as a protecting guardian angel.

Lies came to symbolise Anne's suffering girl-friends and all Jews, just as Moshe's two friends did for him. Seven months after reaching Brussels, Moshe frequently thought and dreamt of his best friend, a boy to whom he had studied Talmud, and about a particularly special girl. On 19/1/1943, he recorded: "When I am doing nothing, my mind starts wandering, her image floats up before my eyes; she appears to me in all her beauty." (66). Remembering these two, who symbolised the whole Jewish race, did not comfort Moshe, but often moved him to uncontrolled tears as he cried: "Where are they? Where is my people, the Chosen People of God" (67).

# Chapter 13

Prophetic Insight

The diarists hoped to outlive the war. Each hoped for an Allied victory, except that Moshe deliberately and repeatedly told himself that such hope was futile, useless, perhaps even a danger. He wrote "one may practically say that it is forbidden to entertain such hope." (55).

Moshe repeatedly told himself that an Allied victory would lull the Jewish people into worldly security and eventually into assimilation. He wrestled with the conviction that an Allied victory would not be true salvation, merely the temptation towards the loss of Jewish identity.

Current trends towards assimilation, especially in America, and the rate of out-marriage there, currently about 45-55%, could decimate American Jewry within two generations. Moshe's fears may well be borne out.

Moshe expressed particular concern about the world-wide influence of Nazi anti-semitic propaganda. He concluded, especially after viewing the movie "Jew Suss", that the Nazis may lose the war but that their poisonous ideology would spread until the whole world was contaminated.

The current spread of neo-nazism, even into Switzerland, Sweden and Denmark, suggest that these fears were very perceptive. Moshe discerned that trusting in a Russian, English or American victory was a danger, in the long term, and that Divine redemption, in the Land of Israel, is the only hope of the Jewish people.

On the other hand Moshe viewed German hegemony and its attendant troubles as `the birth pangs of Messiah', in somewhat the same way that religious Jews in the Soviet Union, in the post war period, have viewed their own sufferings. In both cases it spurred a desire for `shivat Zion': the return to Zion.

At Hanukkah (November 30th, 1942) Moshe actively looked for redemption, a miracle of return to The Land, but by the fifth night of the Festival he had lost all hope of such a miracle as the situation for the Jews deteriorated all around him.

Moshe's conviction that redemption was the Lord's will often wavered from moment to moment. He wrote: "We need supernatural help if the Lord still wishes to save us. If He will not grant us this miracle of salvation, not many Jews will live to take part in our redemption. But the Lord will not be able to forsake His people, undoubtedly He will save us, He must save us" (52) and he continued to pray: "Return us unto Thee, O Lord, and we shall return; renew our days as of old" (50).

By March, 1943, Moshe began to express hatred for the Allies because a German victory would force their redemption, and the end of their exile from the Lord. Moshe's longing for redemption became fused with his desire for `The Homeland': a Zionist redemption and an end to the Diaspora. "Each time I stand to say the Eighteen Benedictions" he wrote on 9/3/1943, "I direct my whole soul to my lovely land, and I see it before my eyes; I see the coast, I see Tel Aviv, Jaffa and Haifa. Then I see Jerusalem, with the Mount of Olives, and I see the Jordan as it flows from Lebanon to the Dead Sea.....And when I pray I do not see my beloved country before my eyes as if my prayer had been rejected and as if I had been praying to the wall" (81-82).

By May 1944, Anne was aware of the growth of anti-semitism in Holland, as the privations of occupation increased and as more gentiles were killed for sheltering Jews. Jews were hated and blamed if, under torture, they gave information that endangered others. While Anne perceived that the Dutch citizenship she coveted may never be possible, she, unlike Moshe, was hardly aware of Eretz Israel as a possible haven, even though Margot's plan was to be a midwife in Palestine.

In contrast to Moshe's anguish of soul, Yitskhok Rudashevski refused to lose heart and wrote with a humour that every Jew would understand. At Purim, on 21st March 1943, he wrote: "We are waiting for the real Purim. Next year we shall eat Hitler tashn" (137).

Although not deluded about the seriousness of their situations the diarists clung to hope wherever possible. Although they oscillated between fear and hope they reverted to the latter as soon as possible, even when hope seemed irrational. Anne, for example, expressed hope in the return of tranquillity, even at the end: "I can feel the sufferings of millions and yet, if I look up to the heavens, I think that it will all come right, that this cruelty too will end, and that peace and tranquillity will return again" (218-219).

# Chapter 14

Jewish Identity

Given the circumstances, it is natural that the young people would wonder about the nature of "Jewishness", and how it was that they were treated as different. Both Yitskhok and Moshe, despite their religious polarity were staunchly proud of their Jewishness. Moshe asserted it by citing the treatment he was receiving as a Jew: "all the troubles directed toward that group of people known as Jews are directed towards me as well" (93).

For each of the diarists, Jewishness was simply life: it was family, community and future. This was not self-conscious or contrived, it was as much part of them as breathing. It was because they were Jewish that they were suffering. There was no escape, not even conversion to Christianity, as Moshe wrote: "It is enough that we are JEWS" (27) and in March 1944 Eva recorded that her father, who had become a Catholic sometime previously, asked her mother, Agi, if she wanted Eva to become a Catholic too. "It doesn't matter to Agi. She is for anything that might help me, but," wrote Eva, "unfortunately there is a Race Law and it doesn't matter what a person's religion is"(67).

Young as these diarists were, each was painfully aware of the humiliation which the Nazis intended to impose upon each and every Jew. Each recorded how being Jewish became stark reality, inescapable ignominy, symbolised by the yellow star. The Nazi requirement for Jews to wear an insignia of their race was so significant that all four diarists record the matter. The wearing of a yellow star might appear, in hindsight, to be a minor disability, when compared with later treatment, yet it was felt, even by the young, to be a major misfortune and a disgrace. Moshe called the star a "Badge of Shame" (24/11/1942), even though he did not wear it, as his family lived with Aryan identity papers.

The Nazi takeover of Hungary occurred very late in the war. Eva noted on 29/3/1944 that they had instituted the wearing of the yellow star and were pedantic about the its size. In Vilna, however, the initial decree of 8/7/1941, was for a yellow circle. This requirement was changed by 2/8/1941 to a yellow star.

On 20/6/1942 Anne listed the wearing of a yellow star first on a list of Anti-Jewish decrees which marked the suffering of the Jews. Anne, who wore the star on the way to the hiding place, wrote that gentiles watching them were aware of its humiliating designation. She wrote: "we got sympathetic looks from people on their way to work. You could see by their faces how sorry they were, they couldn't offer us a lift. The gaudy yellow star spoke for itself" (25). After Anne went into hiding she no longer wore the Jewish insignia, but looked from her vantage point with pity upon those wearing it in the streets.

Yitskhok recorded his initial repulsion and shame. He felt as though each star was a frog sitting on his person. Yet, for him, the humiliation of seeing how fellow Jews demeaned themselves in the ghetto, was much more painful. The 'Badge' was external and did not touch their souls. Unlike the Racz family members who admired Agi's ability to wheedle, cajole or buy what she needed, Yitskhok, with the untarnished scruples of youth, disdained those who used "pull", and ingratiated themselves to gain favours. His most vehement scorn, however, was saved for the Jewish police, of whom he wrote: "I hate them from the bottom of my heart, ghetto Jews in uniforms, and how arrogantly they stride in the boots they have plundered... In me they arouse a feeling compounded of ridicule, disgust and fear" (70). The very next day he wrote: "Jews will dip their hands in the dirtiest and bloodiest work... How great is our misfortune, how great is our shame, our humiliation! Jews help the Germans in their organised, terrible work of extermination" (71).

# Chapter 15

Jewish Education and Practice

In Anne's religious training the emphasis was on freedom rather than regulations. Anne's religious education included systematic reading of the Bible, including the New Testament, use of the prayer book, and the saying of supervised prayers at bed-time.

Her spiritual response was openness of heart and mind, love of God, nature and people. Two quotations represent her embrace of life in all its dimensions. The first deals with faith, the second concerns ideals and her hopes for the future: "My advice is: `Go outside, to the fields, enjoy nature and the sunshine, go out and try to recapture happiness in yourself and in God. Think of all the beauty that's still left in and around you and be happy" (146). "I keep (my ideals) because in spite of everything I still believe that people are really good at heart... I can feel the sufferings of millions and yet, if I look up into the heavens, I think that it will all come right, that this cruelty too will end, and that peace and tranquillity will return again. In the meantime, I must uphold my ideals, for perhaps the time will come when I shall be able to carry them out" (218f).

Moshes' religious practices centred around daily praying, with phylacteries; Talmudic study; and daily Bible study. Eighteen days after commencing his chronicle he wrote: "One of the eternal books - perhaps the only one - that I know is the Divine Bible, particularly the Pentateuch and Prophetic sections. I therefore intend to concentrate on reading the Bible because its importance matches and perhaps even exceeds that of these days" (39).

Moshe found this resolution difficult to carry through, as he had difficulty concentrating and became easily disheartened. "I will force myself to read the whole Bible, and I am sure," he wrote, "that gradually the interest will come. Each day, as I pray, I will ask the Lord to bring me closer to His Book. And perhaps the Lord's promise to Joshua, "And then you shall become wise," will be fulfilled in me." (47).

Eva, the great-granddaughter of a Rabbi, noted in her diary that, in the makeshift hospital (an uncompleted synagogue) the Holy Ark was used to hold bowls, bedpans and pots. Similarly Moshe noted in December, 1942, that pro-Nazi elements in Brussels had repeatedly attempted to burn down the main synagogue.

With dejection Yitskhok simultaneously recorded both his grandmother's disappearance and the fate of the old ghetto synagogue: "Never was there vented on them so much devastation, desolation as now" he wrote; "The old synagogue courtyard is pogromised. Phylacteries, religious books, rags are scatterer under ones feet. Everything in the second ghetto is demolished, broken and abandoned. Everything is pervaded by the despair of those who have been wrenched away from here. The word Ponar (to which they might be deported) hovers among the old ghetto streets" (46).

While Moshe hated the matchmakers, Yitskhok reserved his most acrid condemnation for the Jewish police who `play a comedy with their own tragedy'. He reserved disdain for those, including cantor and rabbi, who attended the impressive and solemn funeral of a ghetto policeman, a "Hero", who fell while performing his duty. Yitskhoh's admiration was reserved for those, of whatever belief, whose behaviour was worthy of admiration.

# Chapter 16



## Emunah

Moshe Flinker gave a definition of faith based on the Hebrew word 'Emunah', a word which incorporates belief (basic biblical virtue and morality), belief in God, in the Jewish people and in The Land (Zion). These four aspects combined together to form a sacred ideal which Moshe chose for the good of his people and their homeland.

Moshe described faith, which does not depend on external objects, as "the Holiest thing in the world." He continued, "faith defines and explains all we ought to be, how we ought to conduct ourselves, and what we ought to believe... The abiding faith we have in our people, our unique people, our eternal people, whose great suffering serves only to intensify its determination and its courage. The faith we possess in our own land which belonged to us once and will belong to us again, the land which was sanctified through our faith in it, and which grants us new strength each and every day. Crowning everything is our faith in the God of our forefathers, the eternal God, our Lord, the Lord of Israel, who has guided and protected us this far, through valleys steep as Sheol, over many a hazardous precipice and through the most terrifying fiery trials" (91).

Such a deep understanding of suffering gave Moshe a profoundly spiritual perspective that differed markedly from the other diarists. Each of them asked the age old questions about Jewish suffering in the light of Jewish chosenness, and about the triumph of evil over good: questions which have characterised Jewish thought since the days of the prophets. In Moshe's writings all questions became penetrating spiritual questions.

Eva, on the other hand, could not find answers to her questions, only excuses. She wrote: "God, its true isn't it, that it is only by accident that you weren't paying attention when they killed Marta, but now you are watching over us?!" (66).

Anne did not find answers either, but she found peace and acceptance. Only twenty days before her deportation she wrote: "It's really a wonder I haven't dropped all my ideals because they seem so absurd and impossible to carry out. Yet, I keep them because in spit of everything I still believe that people are really good at heart ..... I hear the ever approaching thunder, which will destroy us too, I can feel the sufferings of millions and yet, if I look up into the heavens, I think that it will all come right, that this cruelty too will end, and that peace and tranquillity will return again" (218).

Moshe's definition of faith encompasses belief and conduct; abiding faith in the unique and eternal people whose determination and courage grows during great sufferings; faith in the sacred Land will once again belong to them, and principally, faith in the Eternal God of Israel. It is a definition of faith which is entirely appropriate in the Jewish context in which these diaries were written. Moshe wrote of Judaism: "We should never abandon our faith lest we abandon ourselves; our faith will accompany us forever, until by its strength we shall win" (92).

Faith, the inner conviction of a good outcome for themselves, often alluded these youngsters, and understandably so. Yet faith in its wider meanings, faith in a greater or more universal external good, grew and indeed flourished. Each diarist had a distinct understanding of what that greater good could be; a future in the Land of Israel; a future prosperity for the Jewish people; a Divine redemption, the ultimate triumph of goodness. These perceptions were aspects of Moshe's concept of faith, yet all were true and consistent with the individual's world view of Jewish identity, community and culture. Despite their emotional storms and constricted life circumstance, this faith grew rather than wilted.

## FAITH IN GOD

Jewish identity and religion formed a major constraint in the lives of these adolescents, whether their family's religious practice was, like Moshe's, Orthodox; or liberal, like Anne's; or progressive and non-traditional like Eva's; or virtually nominal, like Yitskhok's.

Examining the content of those recorded prayers which expressed the strongest longings of the youngsters, will provide some understanding of their belief. Eva wrote: "God, God sweet God, don't let us die, and let Juszti come back to us! I want so much to live! God it's true, isn't it that it is only by accident that You weren't paying attention when they killed Marta, but you are watching over us?!" (66). This prayer expresses a childlike questioning, so different from Moshe's mature probing. Yet the underlying attitude of trust, and awareness of the goodness of God, comes through.

The prayers Anne recorded centred on issues closest to her heart: repentance of her treatment of her friend Lies, prayers for the protection of those she loved, and thankfulness. Anne believed that God had made her people the way they are (i.e., Jewish) and had never deserted them. Anne's understanding of the nature of God may be glimpsed in the quotation: "God wishes to see people happy amidst the simple beauty of nature" (136).

Anne's was a simplicity of faith which alluded Moshe. His agony was exacerbated by a need to logically account for his people's excessive suffering as punishment for Jewish wickedness. Yet, patently, their sin was not excessive. This logic eventually concludes that God is unjust; but Moshe's alternative explanation, that such a disaster was necessary to drive the Jewish people out of the Diaspora - towards redemption in the Land of Israel - was consistent with his love for the Land, his Messianic hopes and his reading of the prophets.

It is interesting that, while watching women on their way to service on Rosh Hashanah in 1942, Yitskhok recalled how his grandmother had attended synagogue on this day each year. This caused him to muse "Something somehow is missing" (50).

<u>Faith in Zionism</u>

Yitskhok's ideals centred on people and ideologies rather than places; on camaraderie, determination, and youthful vigour. Like Eva, he did not refer to the Jewish Homeland.

Anne, though aware of Palestine through her reading, was not at all preoccupied with it. Unlike Margo, who wished to work as a midwife in the Land, Anne had no such ambition, and only expressed a desire for citizenship of Holland.

As the sufferings of his people progressed Moshe became more passionately Zionistic and more dedicated to the welfare of his beloved Homeland, and his people, of whom he wrote: "we need a country in which we could live at peace as every people in its country" (81). He believed that their suffering would speak for them, grant them merit and guarantee them a future as a nation, the right to return "to our Promised Land, where we shall live as one nation in one country with the one and only true God" (92).

Moshe was depressed about the Jews past failures to listen to the Zionist's pleadings and he wrote: "Those who opposed Zionism bare a frightful sin, and every being that did not go to the land of Israel because of them will be a burden on their conscience" (38).

<u>Faith in the Jewish People</u>

Yitskhok, like Agi Zsolt, was angry that his people were taken like sheep to the slaughter. His triumphant faith was not in the Jewish people, per se, but in the its youth, with its youthful creative spirit, vigour and pride; a youth which worked in the ghetto under the motto 'within walls yet young'. He reiterated the words of the Vilna ghetto teacher, Rokhl Broydo: "When a people has a young generation it is a sign of its progress. We have a youth, its flag is drenched in blood, it is red, but we hold it firmly; the youth in the ghetto, that is the firm bridge to the future" (121).

Eva quoted her Grandmother as saying that she wanted to live because she might live to see a better world. Eva simply wished to live, irrespective of what kind of world it was, even if she was alone, or had to permit the cross-eyed gendarme to kiss her in order to achieve it. Eva's attitude was single minded and simple, uncomplicated with questions of racial intricacies.

Moshe esteemed all Jews as equally valuable, prayed for their redemption and peace, and loved them passionately. This love motivated some extreme and impracticable schemes such as a plan to escape to Palestine or to volunteer for forced labour in Poland or the East. He determined not to leave his people, by trying to flee, even if given the opportunity, but to devote himself to helping his people in their terrible plight.

Anne believed that the day would come when Jews could be people again, and not just 'Jews', and prayed that some of them would survive. Those, who had borne and survived such suffering, would then be held up as examples to others. "Who knows;" she wrote, just two months before her arrest; "it may be our religion from which the world and all peoples learn good, and for that reason and that reason do we suffer now. .... Right through the ages there have been Jews, through all the ages they have had to suffer, but it has made them strong too; the weak fall, but the strong will remain and never go under!" (174).

## Faith in Goodness, Virtues and Ideals

The boys ideas of goodness and virtue centred upon the examples set for them by their teachers. It seems that they found virtue more visible in their mentors than in members of their families.

Moshe was especially influenced by his Hebrew teacher in Holland, Mr Grebel, about whom he wrote little, believing his own soul insufficiently pure to speak of one so "beloved and dear".

Similarly the Vilna Ghetto teachers, some of whom had been Yitskhok's teachers previously, were models of virtue, whose example and ideals he would never forget.

For Eva, greatest virtue was embodied in Juszti, whom Agi described as "the best of us". Juszti helped everyone, never complained, even when she received no wages, and had no life of her own, but lived to devote herself to the family, first as Agi's governess, later as household manager and finally as Eva's governess.

Although Anne was aware of her own failing in virtue, she knew what was right and continually aimed to improve herself, and so achieve goodness. She was clearly aware of the virtues of those she admired, such as her father's longsuffering, and the patient, uncomplaining service of her protectors.

# Chapter 17

Education

As befits the lives of younger teenagers, educational pursuits in the broadest sense, consumed the major portion of their waking hours and in the diaries much detail is provided about current and previous education, the schools attended, subjects studied and the books read.

Education in preparation for the future featured prominently, and gave structure, purpose and dignity to their lives in confinement. Each had ambitions for their future lives. Eva was determined to be a news photographer; Moshe, a statesman in his Homeland; and Anne hoped to be a wife and mother as well as a journalist, and, eventually a famous writer. Yitskhok resisted the temptation to attend the technical school because it led, after four months of training, to employment in one of the workshops, saying: "If for every 100 ghetto children of my age 10 can study, I must be among the fortunate ones, I must take advantage of this. Studying has become even more precious to me than before" (120).

Educational pursuits acted as a de facto barometer of their psychological states. Motivation and energy to study waned as depression set in, and waxed with each resurgence of optimism.

Educational History

After the enactment of the various Jewish Laws in each country major changes in employment, recreation, shopping and schooling were necessary.

Anne was forced to say a tearful farewell to her teacher and leave the Montessori School that she had attended from Kindergarten to grade

6. In 1941, she, and her friend Lies went into Form 1 at the Lyceum, or Jewish Secondary School with an emphasis on the classics. There, of her seven masters and two mistresses. She had most difficulty with Mr. Keptor, the Maths teacher because of her continual chatter.

Anne's final school report card, in mid 1942, was pleasing. Most of her grades were 7 or 8, but with only 5 for Algebra. Yet her parents major interest was not her grades, but her adjustment at school. Anne continued in school until the family went into hiding, and her school books accompanied Anne there - with the intention that Mr Frank would act as teacher.

Eva Heyman also attended a Lyceum. In her last mid-year report card, (February 1944) Eva and another girl, her close friend Aniko or Anni Pajo, were "the best ones in the class". Eva's choice of reading material appears not to have been developed to the mature level of Anne's. Eva recorded having read Jules Verne's "Captain Grant's Children" plus two volumes of "The Little Rebel".

Agi was keen that Eva's French be of a good standard, to assist her to become a journalist. Eva spoke Hungarian and German, although she had "forgotten Romanian". In preference to academic pursuits Eva's priorities, despite her success in schoolwork, favoured athletics, swimming, skating, bike riding, exercise and rhythmics; pastimes for which there were few possibilities in the ghetto.

In The Hague, Moshe had attended public elementary school, and a commercial school for two years, meanwhile having private tuition in Hebrew, with his beloved teacher, Mr Grebel. After being barred from Aryan schools, Moshe attended a Jewish High School, where he continued his commercial studies, until its closure.

Yitskhok's diary provides much rich information about his educational endeavours in the ghetto, but a paucity of data about his previous schooling. His diary begins with the bombing of Vilna, the prompt German invasion, the retreat of the Soviet troops and the closure of his school.

---

## EDUCATION UNDER PERSECUTION and Confinement

Those in the Secret Annex were continually supplied with library books by their protectors. The young people documented their reading on a card index. Anne read a wide assortment: Young People's Annual, plays by Goethe and Schiller, mythology of Greece and Rome, genealogies (especially of the European Monarchies), cinema and theatre magazines, the histories of art, poetry and painting, Dickens, non-fiction such as "The Emperor Charles V", "Galileo Galilei" and "Palestine at the Crossroads" and books in French such as "La Belle Nivernaise", many fictional works including the trilogy "Hungarian Rhapsody" and interesting vogue titles such as "What do you think of the Modern Girl?" and "An Ideal Husband".

In 1943, after a year in hiding, Anne, at the mature age of fourteen, started to write stories. She wrote "Eva's Dream", "Cady's Life", and "Ellen the Fairy". A diary entry reads "...a lovely story called, "Blurr the Explorer". On 17th November, 1942, Anne listed the educational activities in the secret annex as "One written shorthand written lesson per week. English, French, Maths and History at all times"(53). They spoke English, French or Dutch, but no German was permitted, although when particularly angry, Mrs Van Daan abused others, and swore in German.

Anne's greatest desire was to go back to school. She described herself as having a great appetite for learning and she accomplished much study every day. On 27/4/1944 Anne recorded a sample days' activity: "First I translated a piece of Dutch into English...After that, I went through some of Peter the Great's war against Norway (etc.).... After that I landed up in Brazil, read about Bahia tobacco, the abundance of coffee and the one and a half million inhabitants of Rio de Janiro, of Pernambuco and Sao Pasulo, not forgetting the River Amazon; about Negroes, Mulattos, Mezitos, Whites, more than 50 percent of the population being illiterate, and the malaria... I quickly ran through a family tree... Twelve o'clock: in the attic, I continued my programme with the history of the Church.... Just after two.... narrow and broad-nosed monkeys .... the Bible, Noah and the Ark,... After that Charles V. Then with Peter: The Colonel, in English, by Thackeray. Heard my French verbs and then compared the Mississippi with the Missouri" (181-82).

Eva's Lyceum was closed the day the German army invaded the town and the nearby elementary school was later used by the Nazis as a prison. It appears that no attempt at continuing education for Eva was set up, although she continued with reading. Her last words to Mariska, as she gave her the diary for safekeeping, are reported to have been: "Don't be upset, you'll be coming back to us yet you'll see, and I'll go on reading The Sons of the Shonehearted Man to you" (107).

Moshe spent much time on religious and secular education of a very challenging degree of difficulty. He also assisted to educate his four younger sisters, by teaching them French. Moshe was literate in eight languages and taught himself Arabic, from a text-book. His only Arabic dictionary was in German, one of his lesser languages. This immensely difficult assignment was a statement of Zionist faith, as Moshe undertook it in order to prepare himself for a future career as a statesman in his Homeland, to which he, as early as 1942, attached the title ‘Israel'. Of the need for Arabic he wrote: "a large part of the inhabitants of the land of Israel and the surrounding countries speak it. And, in view of my plans, I see that I will need this language more than any that I studied in school. It is obvious that we shall have to live in peace with our brothers, the sons of Ishmael" (47).

Yitskhok, like Anne and Moshe, had a great appetite for study, both for its own sake and as a way of giving meaning and structure to his days. "I long for the studies which sustain us in the Ghetto, without them we become lazier and more negligent;" he wrote. When temporality unable to attend school he wrote: "When in the world will we get back to our studies? When I used to go to my lessons I knew how to divide the days, and the days would fly, and now they drag by for me greyly and sadly" (56).

As ghetto organisation gradually improved, education at many levels was established. On 25/10/42 Yitskhok listed: two kindergartens, three elementary schools, a technical school, Mitlshul (middle school), music school, nursery and dormitory for abandoned children. At one time classes were run in two sessions and Yitskhok attended from 8.45 am until 12 noon. In the afternoons he cooked and cleaned at home, and read from the extensive ghetto library (said to contain 100,000 books). He read in Yiddish, Russian, French and Polish. He was also able to write Hebrew script and to comprehend the humour of adult jokes spoken in a mixture of Hebrew and Yiddish. In the evenings he attended the Ghetto clubs: the history circle, the nature circle, the dramatic circle and the literary circle, which involved both Yiddish literature and folklore. Yitskhok was placed in charge of the creative writing circle under the poet Sutskever, (into whose hands the diary eventually passed). Other evening activities included clandestine meetings of the resurrected Communist Youth Movement plus theatrical productions, exhibitions and evenings of tribute to noted Jewish literary figures and deceased teachers.

Yitskhok recorded that in the ghetto he studied Yiddish, Jewish History, History, Biology, Mathematics, Hebrew, Drawing, Physics, Latin and German. At a later stage, Chemistry and Geography were added.

Yitskhok greatly mourned the passing of his beloved teachers and heroes. An essay in which he eulogised his teacher, Yankev Gershteyn, was chosen for presentation at a memorial to commemorate this mentor. It is preserved in full in his diary.

By far Yitskhok's most significant mentor was the lady teacher Mire Bernshteyn, who was his friend, his teacher and dedicated leader of their Pioneer Youth activities.

As the mood of sadness, which Yitskhok often described, increasingly pervaded the Vilna ghetto, the boy sought greater refuge in intellectual pursuits and studies. He became academic and detached, as an observer and recorder of many aspects of the ghetto experience. Yet occasionally, he became aware of the irony of this detachment, when the tragedy of the human drama surfaced and imposed itself over objective analysis.

# Chapter 18

Lessons

Of the limited quantity of original written material from the pen of Jewish victims of the Shoah, the stories of these four teenagers, while not unique, are exceedingly valuable. They provide us with a telescope to look back more than half a century into the past, and a microscope to look closely upon the daily lives of people under extremes of threat and persecution.

In these days when Holocaust denial spreads its web of deceptive lies worldwide we must remember that each diary was brought into the light by friends and close family members who could attest to the events described and who knew of the diligence with which the diary was kept.

After the war it was Anne's beloved father who published her writings from the diary which he himself had given her on her thirteenth birthday. Esther Flinker, Moshe's older sister, then about twenty years old, took possession of Moshe's diary along with the remaining family possessions; while Yitskhok's cousin Sore deliberately searched for his writings. It was the faithful Mariska into whose hands Eva committed both her pet bird and her diary, who kept the book until Agi's return.

The authenticity of the "Diary of Anne Frank", a symbol of the nobility of Jewish youth, has been slanderously and viciously attacked, the Dutch government having gone to considerable pains to prove its bona fides. These four diaries are, however, representative of a wider selection of works and fortunately no-one has had the motivation, time or money to attempt to undermine them all. Since the first edition of this book was written in 1994, author Lauren Holliday has edited "Children's Wartime Diaries: Secret Writings from the Holocaust and World War II" (1995) which contains the writings of twenty-three children from ten to eighteen years of age who wrote during those terrible years; although it does not include Anne Frank's long work.

Each individual life-story represents a responses to the impending deportation of their authors, a unique yet shared Holocaust environment but set within four different national backgrounds. In every case, given the limits of translation, the material must stand as written, because the authors' meaning cannot be expanded upon, revised nor explained. None of the four teenagers survived their Holocaust experience.

Each diarist was dramatically and painfully aware of the fate of their fellow Jews, a fate their families were desperately trying to avoid; although, at times, Moshe did repress that knowledge. Each identified painfully with the sufferings of others, and of the whole Jewish people.

Each of the diarists consciously attempted to make sense of the issue of their persecution, and to construct philosophical and pragmatic reasons to explain it. Given their paucity of data, and their relative immaturity, this was a very difficult quest.

These teenagers shared a passionate desire and a will to live, and actively planned for their future. Their youthful optimism was demonstrated by their dedication to academic pursuits, as well as signifying a love of learning for its own sake. They maintained greater hope and optimism, even greater zeal, than their circumstances logically warranted.

Their active intellectual capacities were constantly engaged in thinking about a wide range of complex and challenging issues; more complex and analytic than any adult family member realised. Although more limited than adults in the breadth of their experiences, the thoughts of these young people were no less wide ranging and complex, and their emotions were not more shallow. These facts were often poorly perceived by the relevant adults; as Anne Frank wrote: "Who could imagine what goes on in the soul of a young 13 year old girl" (120). The adults appear to have been unaware of just how complex the thoughts and feelings of these adolescents were.

Each diarist's individual search for answers was conducted within a total context of Jewishness; Jewish family, social, and religious context. It did not occur to them that there were alternative world views; only alternative answers to the appalling questions 'why?' and 'how?'. It was as Jews that they were being hunted and Nazi ideology ensured that Jewish racial identity was their only relevant existential reality.

It was as Jews that they had to try to make sense of it all, but they were people first; particularly emotionally vulnerable and needy young people who endured "long dark nights of the soul", often on the margins of serious depression and other psychiatric disorders. For the duration of their confinement, each engaged in a primary but often unrequited quest for affection, affirmation and love. They searched hungrily, though often unsuccessfully, within the circles of their Faith, families or friends. At times, in this search, they were often only sustained by fantasies, and by strong memories of those they had once loved. They were upheld by hope, purpose, positive memories, and the devotion of those gentiles who gave a little kindness, or who risked everything to help them.

It is clear, ultimately, that all of these teenagers, especially the two girls, were able to give more of the love for which they hungered to their family members, and to their people and kindred far away, than either they, or the adults around them, were conscious that they possessed.

This was borne out during their imprisonment. When Eva's cousin Marica died in Eva's arms it did not destroy her vibrant spirit. Anne's sister Margot, similarly died in Anne's arms, while both were suffering from typhus. These girls loved and cared for others to the very end.

It is also interesting that it was the girls who benefited most from the selfless devotion of gentiles, primarily gentile women. While ultimately unable to save the lives of their charges, Eva's story is also Juszti's and Mariska's story; and Anne's story is also Eli's, Meip's and Mr Kraler's and Mr Koophius'; these two men being jailed by the Nazis, for their good deeds.

Love was a feature of their lives to the end. Eva remained close to her cousin Marcia, both in the ghetto and then in their destination, Auschwitz, where they arrived on D-Day (6th June, 1944). Marcia died in Eva's arms. Shortly afterwards Eva herself was sent to the gas chambers during the last selection of the notorious Dr Mengele. He personally pushed Eva onto the transport truck, after discovering where a compassionate woman doctor was making yet another unsuccessful attempt to conceal her.

Agi and Bela Zolt escaped from the ghetto with the help of a gentile woman, and they eventually gained admission to Switzerland. Bela died in 1949 at the early age of 51. Agi, unable to sustain her despair, took her own life. Her body was found lying beside a photograph of Eva.

Anne Frank, with all of the occupants of the Secret Annexe, was part of the last transport of Dutch Jews to leave Westerbork transit camp for Auschwitz. Here Mr Van Daan was the first to die in the gas chambers. Only Mr Otto Frank survived the war, being liberated from Auschwitz by the Soviet army on 27/1/1945. Anne and her sister Margot remained inseparable, first in Auschwitz and later in Bergen-Belsen, where they both contracted typhus, dying within a few days of each other. Their mother, Eva Frank, died in Birkenau on 6/1/1945, of malnutrition and a broken spirit. Peter Van Daan died in Mauthhausen, Germany, after barely surviving the Death March from Auschwitz, Poland.

The question of life and death cannot be relinquished without saying that Yitskhok was taken with his family from the Vilna Ghetto to the dreaded valley of mass slaughter, Ponar. Only his cousin, Sore, made an amazing escape.

Moshe's family, Like Anne's, was betrayed to the Nazis by an informer. Of the nine imprisoned in Auschwitz, Mr and Mrs Flinker and Moshe perished. Amazingly the other children survived.

It is selfless love: live of one Jew for another, and the unconditional altruism of the 'Righteous From Among the Nations', 10,000 of whom have been honoured by Yad Vashem, which is the only light in the gross darkness which was the Shoah. Many of those who tried to save Jewish lives are unknown, many perished along with those they tried in vain to help. Those whose names are known are honoured by the planting of a tree and the presentation of a medal; but for the many gentiles whose deeds are still unknown there is a special sculpture on the Hill of Remembrance but their names are recorded Elsewhere. "For whoever saves one soul, is as one who saves the world."

The failure of the nations to act in any concerted way is a blot on the conscience of mankind. At the Evian Conference, in July, 1938, when Hitler offered the Jews to the world for resettlement, only a few nations agreed to accept a few thousand. Australia's delegation and the United States and Canada refused to take any (Arad et al. (eds), 1988, 128f). New Zealand cited economic problems for its inability to accept immigrants. With shame the response of Australia's representative is recorded: "we have no real racial problem, we are not desirous of importing one".

Tribute must be paid to the Dominican Republic which volunteered to do more than its share, and Britain, which eventually accepted more Jewish refugees than Canada, South Africa, Uruguay, Spain and Switzerland put together. Britain eventually accepted 10,000 unaccompanied children who arrived on 'Kindertransport' ships between Kristallnacht and the outbreak of war. One woman was pivotal to these rescues. Mrs Wijsmuller-Meijer, who is credited by Yad Vashem with personally saving about ten thousand children. Her indefatigable efforts prove to us that one individual can indeed make a difference!!

Each of these teenagers' diaries demonstrates literary talent, intelligence, and youthful vigour and each personal story is extremely interesting. When faced with these facts; the literary talents and obvious intelligence and wisdom of these four, while yet so young, we ask the shattering question: How much, how very much has the world lost, how much the poorer will this Earth always be, through every generation, because evil men triumphed when good men did nothing?

WHAT LESSONS HAS MANKIND learnt from this?

Something - perhaps?

Memorial to the rescue of Danish Jewry, Yad Vashem

THERE IS A LITTLE BLUE row-boat at Yad Vashem, donated by the People of Denmark. Near it an inscription informs us of its story, a story which shows that somewhere in the world everyone, from the king (Christian X) down to the village fisher-folk, cooperated with the rescue venture and/or treated the Jews with respect:

The inscription says: "During World War II the Danish People succeeded in frustrating Nazi Germany's intentions of deporting Denmark's 8,000 Jews to death camps in the east. The deportations, which were to be part of the 'final solution' for the destruction of European Jewry, was set in Denmark for the 1st of October, 1943. A courageous rescue operation was carried out by the members of the Danish underground which assisted 7,200 Jews to escape to Sweden. This boat smuggled Jews from the coast of Denmark near the town of Gilleleje to waiting fishing boats at sea, continued their journey to Sweden. The Boat has been placed here to commemorate the 40th anniversary of the rescue of Danish Jewry. The Jewish people will forever remember this noble deed. October 1983. Tishri, 5744."

PLATE 5 A BOAT USED to smuggle Jews from Denmark to Sweden, during the Holocaust. (Exhibited at the Yad Vashem Museum)

Photo by Johnathon Widen (in 2008) using pseudonym of אני יצרתי

Plate 6.

Memorial at Yad Vashem,

A gift from Poland.

Photo: D. Campbell.

Nearby, also in Yad Vashem is a new memorial, one which tells a different story. This one was recently donated by the people of Poland, and it commemorates not those who were saved from deportation, but those who were not. This memorial is an original German railway cattle truck, with its original number. It originated in "Munchen" (Munich) but its final resting place was a rail siding in Poland. Like those who, like a hundred cattle, were crowded into it, this timber crate on wheels made a one-way trip "to the East". Here it remained, abandoned until the fall of communism, until Poles were free to review their past.

These two memorials remind us of two ways of responding to the threat of persecution of all minority groups, and to the survival of the Jewish people. To go along with terror, or to stand silently by is easier. To act righteously in times of danger is difficult, it is not natural. It is much easier to go along with terror, to meekly obey orders (as hundreds of bureaucrats and railway employees did), or to be silent bystanders.

Although we may not be living in the middle of a racial crisis at the moment this issue must be considered by both nations and individuals. Given the current political situation in much of the world, it may not be long before you and I, and our nation, face the challenge of such a crisis, even though surely we ask: have not the Jewish people suffered enough in my lifetime?

Those who train themselves to think of others are better prepared to stand the test in the day of trouble. Those who pre-determine their priorities, who pre-set their hearts on a true course, may know how they will respond.

From the Silence, the voices of our four young diarists ask:

"Would YOU have helped me to lived?"

# BIBLIOGRAPHY

FLINKER, Moshe

"Young Moshe's Diary: Spiritual Torment of a Jewish Boy in Nazi Europe."

Yad Vashem and the Board of Jewish Education

Jerusalem, 1971.

Used with the kind consent of Yad Vashem.

FRANK, Anne

"The Diary of Anne Frank"

Pan Books

London, 1989.

Now in the public domain.

Heyman, Eva

"The Diary of Eva Heyman: Child of the Holocaust"

Yad Vashem and Shapolsky Publishers

New York, 1988.

Used with the kind consent of Yad Vashem.

Rudashevski, Yitskhok

"Diary of the Vilna Ghetto: June 1941-April 1943"

Beit Lohamei Hagettaot

Naharia, 1973.

Used with the kind consent of Beit Lohamei Hagettaot.

"Documents on the Holocaust.

Selected Sources on the Destruction of the Jews of Germany and Austria, Poland, and the Soviet Union."

Editors: Y. Arad, Y. Gutman, A. Margaliot.

Yad Vashem and Pergamon Press

Oxford, 1987.

Documents in the public domain.

www.ingramcontent.com/pod-product-compliance
Lightning Source LLC
Chambersburg PA
CBHW071228130726
47998CB00002B/878